Tilt-a-whirl

Melanie Dreyer

BookLeaf Publishing

India | USA | UK

Presentation by *BookLeaf Publishing*

Web: www.bookleafpub.com

E-mail: info@bookleafpub.com

ISBN: 9789360948412

First edition 2024

*I dedicate this book to my loving husband
who has to put up with all the madness.*

Typewriter

It has been years since I picked you
Writing use to be all I knew
I miss the way the pen fits in my hand
Writing everything down without demand
Now its typing and technology
Writing deserves my sincere apology

Cake

Everyday I wake
Wishing I could eat cake
But its laundry and dishes
And lots of broom swishes

Bedtime

In the night
I start my fight
Tossing and turning
For dreamland i'm yearning
Through the clouds of imagination
Looking for my mental creations

Me

Horrorcore and gore
Is one I love and adore
But I aint that kind of clown
When I decide to throw down
I'm peace, love, unity, respect
Every so often I need to be checked

Addiction

Puff puff off my vape
Nicotine i cannot escape
You twirl my mind
Pretending to be kind
Not another disorder
But just another border
I can try to cross over
Or i can find a clover

My Mom

Without a doubt
I gotta give a shout out
To my Mom
Who is the bomb
She raised me well
I tried not to give her hell
She's quick and clean
Rarely is she mean

Puppy Ears

Things start to look up,
My ears droop like a pup,
Never able to get ahead,
There is always dread,
Fear for the worst,
It's like I've been cursed,
Always looking for a silver lining,
I need that star to be shining.

Finding Time

Finding time to write you
Is a whim out of the blue
Poetry who knew
It's in review
Times up! It's Due!
Keeping True
Progress is hard to accrue
When life bounds to subdue

Chewy

Chewy my pet
I am happy we met
Your barks are cute
But you are mostly mute
Licks of love
Sent from above
Life with you
I can ensue

Feline

Star you are annoying
and very coying
constantly toying
sometimes you're enjoying
but overly cloying

Andie

My eldest child
You drive me wild
You made me a mother
With so much to discover
Through thick and thin
We've taken it on the chin
Together forever
Through every endeavour

Kevin

My sensitive son
You were the one
who changed my world
like a meteor hurled
With lightning speed
I'm sure you'll succeed

Bart

Trouble with a sunshine smile
Leaving toys in organized piles
My autistic pup
With an artsy hup
Your hearts so big
The girls will dig

MW

Oh my unruly child
Definitely beguiled
You scare me the most
With your personality boast
There is no start or stop
I can only glop

Husby

To the love of my life
There is no strife
Loving you has been easy
Although that may sound cheesy
You should be proud
With your brain in the cloud
Heart on your sleeve
I'll never leave

Unapologetic Shopping Mother

Dropping a jar on the floor
Of the grocery store
How embarrassing of me
I try to tidy up and flee
Juggling four kids
Heaven forbids
The looks I'll receive
Like snot on a sleeve
I pay for my goods
Just as I should
My head held up high
As I let my middle finger fly

Hell

Doing laundry is a bore
It clearly is not my favorite chore
Washing, drying, and folding cloth
Hoping I did not just see a moth
Loads and loads pile on in
This is how every morning begins

The Cramps

You scribble up my insides
You tear me apart in strides
You rip up my heart
You throw nuclear darts
You make me plead for mercy
You make me eat Hershey's

Breakfast

I tell you I never want you
Maybe once in a while out of blue
But when I do
It's a little taboo
A little pastry puff
To call my bluff

Lunch

The most annoying time of day
Looking for a meal that will slay
Never finding what I want
Leaving me with just a croissant
My stomach grumbles with dissatisfaction
I give up instead of taking action

Dinner

A heavy meal awaits to be eaten
Something savory rather than sweeten
A meal I can eat anytime of the day
This is my typical way
Breakfast, lunch, or dinner
I find it a real winner